RHINE RIVER

CRUISE

TRAVEL GUIDE 2024-2025

Ultimate Companion for First-Time Visitors to
Discover the Charms of Its Cultural History,
Vineyards, Cuisine, and Other Unforgettable
Destinations

Rick M. Driver

Disclaimer

Table Of Contents

Map of Strasbourg Along Rhine River

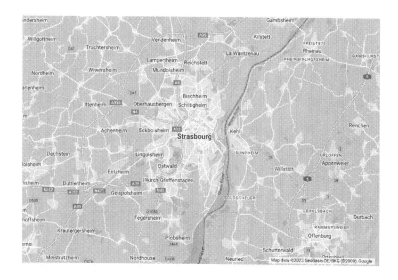

Map of Rhine River, Basel, Switzerland

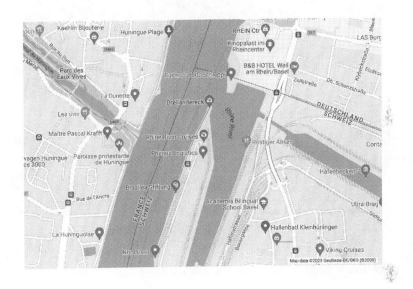

Introduction

Imagine being in the heart of Europe, where the past mixes seamlessly with stunning views. That's the Rhine River for you—a place filled with history and beauty that you can explore endlessly. The "Rhine River Cruise Travel Guide 2024-2025" is your go-to companion for this adventure, carefully made to help you discover the culture, history, and wonders along the Rhine.

As you read through this guide, it's not just about
telling you where to go; it's about painting a picture
beyond the usual. You'll find detailed plans that take
you to castles from medieval times sitting on hills
covered in vineyards. There are also charming
villages that feel like they're from another era and
bustling cities with a modern vibe. Each part of the
guide opens a door into what the Rhine has to offer,
with tips on where to get the best views of sunsets
and the secret spots that make riverside towns come
alive.

This "Rhine River Cruise Travel Guide 2024-2025"
isn't just a list of travel ideas. It's like a storybook
that immerses you in the breathtaking beauty of the
Rhine. The pages are filled with pictures showing
off historic landmarks, beautiful landscapes, and the
friendly faces that make the region special. The
guide smoothly connects the past with today, giving

you a deep understanding of the Rhine's cultural richness.

But there's more to it than just pretty scenes. This guide spills the beans on why a river cruise is such a fantastic idea. Think luxurious places to stay, delicious dining experiences, and custom-made trips for travelers who want both relaxation and culture. It even spills the secrets of getting exclusive access to some of the best wineries along the famous Rhine vineyards.

The "Rhine River Cruise Travel Guide 2024-2025" is more than a guide; it's like a friend helping you create memories. You'll get practical tips on navigating the river, understanding local traditions, and mingling with the lively communities. Whether you've traveled a lot or it's your first river cruise, this guide turns your Rhine River journey into a story that's uniquely yours, filled with the special charm of the region.

Become a river explorer with the "Rhine River Cruise Travel Guide 2024-2025," your ticket to the magic of the Rhine. Dive into a journey where each page reveals a new chapter in your personal Rhine River adventure, leaving you with memories that will stick with you forever.

Chapter 1: Overview Of Rhine River Cruise

History of The Rhine River

The Rhine River has a long and storied history that dates back thousands of years. It is one of the most important rivers in Europe and has played a crucial role in the development of the continent.

The history of the Rhine River can be traced back to ancient times, with evidence of human settlements along its banks dating back to the Neolithic period. The river has been a vital trade route since at least the Roman era, when it was used to transport goods and people across the region. The Romans also built a series of fortifications along the river to protect their empire from invading tribes.

During the Middle Ages, the Rhine River became even more important as a trade route, connecting the cities and towns of Europe and facilitating the exchange of goods and ideas. The river was also a key strategic asset, with numerous castles and fortresses built along its banks to control access to the waterway.

In the 19th century, the Rhine River became a hotbed of industrial activity, with the development of steam-powered boats and the construction of canals and locks to improve navigation. The river also played a crucial role in the unification of Germany, as it served as a natural border between various German states.

The 20th century saw the Rhine River become a symbol of European unity and cooperation. The signing of the Treaty of Versailles in 1919 established the Rhine as an international waterway, and the creation of the European Coal and Steel Community in 1951 further solidified its importance as a symbol of European unity.

Today, the Rhine River continues to be an important trade route, with millions of tons of goods transported along its length each year. It is also a popular tourist destination, with its picturesque landscapes, historic castles, and charming towns attracting visitors from around the world.

Culture of The Rhine River Region

A lengthy history of human settlement and interaction has produced the rich and diversified culture of the Rhine River region. The river has been essential to trade and communication for thousands of years, resulting in a blending of many customs and cultures.

The area was greatly impacted by the Romans, who left behind artifacts such as the Roman bridge in Trier and shaped the design of towns and cities. The numerous castles and fortresses along the river, which functioned as both defensive fortifications and power centers, are clear indications that the Middle Ages also had an impact. Even now, several of these medieval buildings still survive and draw tourists.

The area is well-known for its colorful folk customs and celebrations, which honor yearly occasions like wine and harvest festivals. The region's agricultural heritage and close relationships to the soil are reflected in these celebrations.

Particularly in Alsace, Germany's Rhine Valley, and the Moselle Valley, wine production is a notable characteristic. Renowned wines like Riesling and Pinot Noir are produced in abundance from the vineyards. Visitors frequently participate in wine tasting festivals and tours, which provide an opportunity to savor some of Europe's best wines in scenic settings.

The Rhine River region is home to a flourishing modern arts sector in addition to its historical and cultural components. Vibrant artistic communities can be found in cities like Cologne, Düsseldorf, and Strasbourg, where traditional and modern art is exhibited in theaters, galleries, and music venues.

Landscapes and Vineyards

The landscapes along the Rhine River are renowned for their scenic beauty, diverse geography, and historic charm. The river winds its way through several European countries, offering a tapestry of landscapes, picturesque villages, and terraced vineyards. Here's a detailed exploration of the landscapes and vineyards along the Rhine River:

Landscapes Along the Rhine River

1. Rhine Gorge (Rhine Canyon):

The Rhine Gorge, also known as the "Romantic Rhine," is a particularly captivating section of the river. This narrow gorge is flanked by steep, vine-covered slopes, medieval castles, and charming villages. The Lorelei Rock, a legendary slate rock formation, adds to the mystique of this region.

2. Rhine Valley:

The broader Rhine Valley encompasses a range of landscapes. In the Upper Rhine, the river flows through the scenic Alsace region, known for its vineyards, rolling hills, and charming half-timbered houses. As it progresses, the valley widens, revealing fertile plains and meandering sections that pass through vibrant cities like Strasbourg and Basel.

3. Vineyard Terraces:

The Rhine is surrounded by terraced vineyards, especially in the Middle Rhine and Upper Rhine regions. These vineyards are meticulously arranged on the steep slopes along the riverbanks. The terracing not only maximizes sunlight exposure for grape cultivation but also adds to the aesthetic appeal of the landscape.

4. Rhine Gau (Rhine Region):

The Rhine Gau refers to the broader region surrounding the Rhine. It is characterized by a mix of vine-covered hills, fertile agricultural land, and dense forests. This region has been shaped by centuries of human settlement, and picturesque towns and castles dot the landscape.

5. Rheingau Wine Region:

The Rheingau, one of the most famous wine regions along the Rhine, is known for its vineyards producing high-quality Riesling wines. The landscape here is dominated by orderly rows of grapevines on south-facing slopes overlooking the river. Historic wine estates, medieval abbeys, and charming wine villages contribute to the cultural richness of the area.

Vineyards Along the Rhine River

1. Rheingau Vineyards:

The Rheingau region is renowned for its Riesling vineyards. The south-facing slopes along the river benefit from optimal sunlight exposure, creating favorable conditions for grape cultivation. Visitors can explore vineyards, participate in wine tastings, and enjoy panoramic views of the Rhine.

2. Mosel Wine Region:

While the Mosel River is a tributary of the Rhine, its wine region is noteworthy. The Mosel Valley is characterized by steep terraced vineyards along the riverbanks, producing exceptional white wines. The quaint villages and medieval castles add to the charm of this wine region.

3. Middle Rhine Vineyards:

The Middle Rhine region features picturesque vineyards on the slopes overlooking the river. The combination of a favorable climate, slate soil, and the river's moderating influence contributes to the production of distinctive wines. Vineyard tours often include visits to historic wine estates.

4. Alsace Wine Region:

The Alsace region, through which the Rhine flows, is renowned for its aromatic white wines. The vineyards in Alsace are characterized by a patchwork of small plots, each contributing to the region's diverse wine offerings. The landscape here is complemented by charming villages with colorful half-timbered houses.

5. Wachau Wine Region (Danube-Rhine Connection):

As the Rhine and Danube rivers are connected via the Main-Danube Canal, the Wachau region in Austria becomes accessible. This region along the Danube is known for its vineyards, particularly those producing Grüner Veltliner and Riesling wines. The terraced vineyards are set against a backdrop of rolling hills and medieval architecture.

Course of The Rhine River

The Rhine River traces a northward course from its sources in Switzerland through five additional countries before veering westward into the North Sea. Its origins lie in two principal sources within

Switzerland— the Anterior Rhine in Tomasee and the Posterior Rhine in Tamin, both situated in Graubünden. The 76-kilometer-long Anterior Rhine originates from Lake Toma at an altitude of 2,344 meters and converges with the 64-kilometer-long Posterior Rhine in Reichenau, forming the Rhine River. Despite being approximately 5% shorter, the Posterior Rhine boasts a significantly larger volume.

As the Rhine approaches Chur, it changes direction to the north, flowing through the Rhine Valley and serving as the boundary between Switzerland and Liechtenstein, followed by Switzerland and Austria. This segment, spanning about 90 kilometers, sees an elevation decrease from 600 meters to 400 meters. Shortly thereafter, the river creates an inland delta, discharging into Lake Constance, Austria. This area is characterized by straight, fortified banks designed to manage flooding. The inland delta at Lake

Constance's entrance is a critical bird sanctuary and nature reserve.

High Rhine

Exiting Lake Constance through the Untersee arm, the Rhine proceeds toward Basel, constituting the High Rhine (Hochrhein) section. A significant juncture occurs as the Aare, the Rhine's major tributary, joins, doubling the river's discharge rate to approximately 1,000 cubic meters per second. Flowing west from Lake Constance, the Rhine descends to about 252 meters near the Rhine Falls, then shifts northward in Basel, marking the Rhine Knee. Portions of the High Rhine run along the Switzerland-Germany border, while others remain entirely within Switzerland.

Upper Rhine

The High Rhine concludes at the Rhine Knee in Basel, where the river changes direction from west to north. The Central Bridge marks the demarcation between the High and Upper Rhine. The Upper Rhine continues its northward course for approximately 300 kilometers through the Upper Rhine plains, receiving contributions from tributaries such as the Ill River, Neckar, and Main, the latter joining near Mainz. Exiting the Rhine Valley through the Mainz Basin, the Upper Rhine forms the border between Germany (Baden-Württemberg) and France (Alsace). In the 19th century, before its straightening, the Upper Rhine exhibited expansive meanders in its floodplains.

Middle Rhine and Lower Rhine

The Middle Rhine section extends between Bingen an Rhein and Bonn in Germany, encompassing approximately 145 kilometers. As the river flows through the Rhine Gorge, created by erosion, it descends to about 50.4 meters above sea level, navigating the Rhenish Slate Mountains, with the Eifel and Hunsruck ranges to the left and Westerwald and Taunus to the right. Main tributaries, Mosella and Lahn Rivers, join near Koblenz.

Transitioning into the Lower Rhine, the river enters the North German Plains, with the elevation dropping to 12 meters. Fed by Lippe and Ruhr, this section flows through North Rhine-Westphalia, passing the Rhine-Ruhr region, Germany's most densely populated metropolitan area, and crossing the Uerdingen line near Krefeld. The Rhine then turns westward, entering Dutch territory, where it branches into several distributaries, including Waal and Lek. Teaming up with Scheldt and Meuse Rivers, the Rhine shapes the Rhine-Meuse-Scheldt delta, the largest river delta in Europe, covering an expansive 25,347 square kilometers.

Ports And Destinations

A Rhine River cruise offers a unique and enchanting way to explore some of the most beautiful and historic destinations in Europe. As the river flows through six countries, there are numerous ports and destinations that can be visited along the way.

One popular starting point for Rhine River cruises is Basel, Switzerland. This vibrant city is known for its rich cultural heritage, stunning architecture, and world-class art museums. Visitors can explore the

Old Town, visit the Basel Minster, and stroll along the banks of the Rhine before embarking on their cruise.

As the cruise continues northward, passengers will have the opportunity to visit the charming town of Strasbourg, France. Situated on the border between France and Germany, Strasbourg is famous for its picturesque canals, half-timbered houses, and the stunning Strasbourg Cathedral. The city also boasts a unique blend of French and German influences, making it a fascinating destination for cultural exploration.

Another highlight of a Rhine River cruise is the city of Cologne, Germany. Home to the iconic Cologne Cathedral, this historic city offers a perfect mix of old-world charm and modern sophistication. Visitors can explore the cobblestone streets of the Old Town, sample local beers in traditional beer halls, and take in panoramic views of the city from the cathedral's spires.

As the cruise approaches the Netherlands, passengers will have the opportunity to visit the picturesque town of Kinderdijk, known for its iconic windmills and UNESCO World Heritage-listed landscape. This serene and idyllic destination offers a glimpse into traditional Dutch life and showcases the country's iconic windmill heritage.

Finally, the Rhine River cruise culminates in the bustling port city of Rotterdam, Netherlands. As one of the largest and busiest ports in the world, Rotterdam is a vibrant metropolis with a rich maritime history. Visitors can explore modern architectural marvels, such as the Cube Houses and Erasmus Bridge, or delve into the city's cultural offerings at museums and galleries.

In addition to these key destinations, a Rhine River cruise also offers opportunities to explore smaller towns, vineyards, and historic castles along the way. Whether it's sampling fine wines in the Rhine Valley or admiring medieval fortresses perched on hilltops, there is no shortage of captivating experiences to be had on a Rhine River cruise. With its diverse array of ports and destinations, a journey along the Rhine River promises an unforgettable blend of history, culture, and natural beauty.

In Summary:

The Rhine River, one of Europe's most prominent waterways, flows through six countries, shaping a course that encompasses a range of culturally rich and historically significant cities. Here is a list of Ports of Call situated along the Rhine River:

Switzerland:

- Basel

France:

- Strasbourg

Germany:

- Cologne

Netherlands:

- Rotterdam

Additionally, the Rhine River cruise offers opportunities to explore smaller towns, vineyards, and historic castles, providing a diverse array of experiences along the journey. Whether savoring fine wines in the Rhine Valley or marveling at medieval fortresses perched on hilltops, the cruise promises an unforgettable blend of history, culture, and natural beauty throughout its ports and destinations.

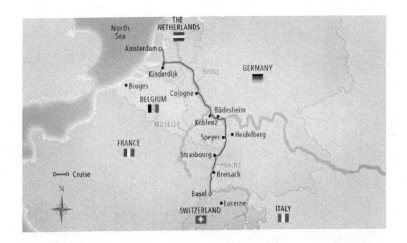

Geography

The Rhine River stands as one of Europe's major waterways, holding the distinction of being the continent's third-longest river. Originating in the Swiss Alps, it embarks on a journey that spans approximately 764 miles (1230 kilometers) before converging into the North Sea. The river's two primary sources, the Anterior Rhine in Tomasee and the Posterior Rhine in Tamin, both located in Switzerland's Graubünden region, blend at Reichenau to form the mighty Rhine.

Winding its way northward, the Rhine traverses various landscapes, making significant turns and passing through several notable cities. The river's course takes it through Switzerland, forming natural boundaries with Liechtenstein and Austria before crossing into Germany. As it flows through Germany, it touches upon cities like Basel, Mainz, and Cologne, shaping the picturesque landscapes of the Rhine Valley and Rhine Gorge.

The Rhine's journey through Germany unfolds in three key segments: the High Rhine (Hochrhein) from Lake Constance to Basel, the Upper Rhine from Basel to Mainz, and the Middle and Lower Rhine from Mainz to the North Sea. Along this course, the river is joined by various tributaries, such as the Aare, Moselle, and Lahn, each contributing to the dynamic character of the Rhine.

The Rhine serves as a vital watercourse for the countries it touches, acting as a key channel for trade, transportation, and cultural exchange. Six nations share connections with the Rhine or are part of its extensive watershed. Switzerland, Liechtenstein, Austria, Germany, France, and the Netherlands all have ties to this iconic river. The Rhine's watershed extends into regions of Switzerland, Austria, Liechtenstein, Germany, and France, contributing to its influence on diverse landscapes and ecosystems.

Water Temperature

The water temperature of the Rhine river varies throughout the year and is influenced by a variety of factors, including the weather, the flow of the river, and the surrounding landscape.

During the winter months, the water temperature of the Rhine river tends to be quite cold, especially in the alpine regions of Switzerland. In these areas, the water temperature can drop to near freezing, particularly in the high-altitude sections of the river. As the river flows through Germany and France, the water temperature remains relatively cool, but it begins to gradually warm up as it passes through the Rhine Valley.

In the spring and summer months, the water temperature of the Rhine river becomes more moderate and comfortable for recreational activities such as swimming, boating, and fishing. In the warmer months, the water temperature can range from around 15 to 20 degrees Celsius (59 to 68 degrees Fahrenheit) in the lower elevations of the river. However, in the higher elevations and mountainous regions, the water temperature may still be quite chilly even during the summer.

The water temperature of the Rhine river is also affected by human activities, such as industrial and agricultural runoff, as well as the regulation of water flow for hydroelectric power generation. These factors can impact the overall temperature and quality of the water in certain areas of the river.

Flora And Fauna Of The Rhine River

The Rhine River harbors diverse flora and fauna due to its varied landscapes. Its surroundings offer a rich, fertile environment, supporting a wide array of plant and animal species. The river and its diverse habitats contribute to the thriving ecosystem, creating a home for many plants and animals.

Flora:

The banks of the Rhine river are lined with a variety of plant life, including trees, shrubs, and other vegetation. In the upper reaches of the river, particularly in the alpine regions of Switzerland, coniferous forests dominate the landscape. Here, you can find species such as spruce, fir, and pine trees, as well as alpine meadows filled with wildflowers and grasses.

As the river flows through Germany and France, the landscape changes, and deciduous forests become more common. Trees such as oak, beech, and maple can be found along the riverbanks, providing habitat for a wide range of wildlife. Additionally, wetlands and marshes along the Rhine river support a variety of aquatic plants, including reeds, cattails, and water lilies.

Fauna:

The Rhine river is teeming with a diverse array of wildlife, both in the water and on land. The river supports numerous fish species, including trout, salmon, pike, and perch. These fish are an important part of the river's ecosystem and are also prized by anglers.

Birds are also abundant along the Rhine river, with species such as herons, ducks, swans, and kingfishers making their homes in the wetlands and forests that line the riverbanks. The river also provides a vital migratory route for many bird species, making it an important area for birdwatching and conservation.

Mammals such as otters, beavers, and deer can be found in the wooded areas surrounding the Rhine river, while smaller creatures like frogs, toads, and insects are also plentiful in the wetlands and marshes.

In addition to its natural inhabitants, the Rhine river is also home to a variety of domesticated animals, including livestock that graze in the meadows and fields along the riverbanks.

Chapter 2: Getting Started

When to Cruise The Rhine River

Due to perfect weather and little crowds, late April to early June and early September to early October are generally regarded as the finest times to cruise the Rhine River; however, these dates also tend to have higher cruise fees. Having said that, choosing the right time to go on a Rhine River cruise mostly depends on personal weather preferences.

In summary:

June through August is peak tourist season; other seasons include spring and autumn, which have milder temperatures and are referred to as shoulder seasons; November and December are ideal for traveling the Rhine to visit the traditional Christmas markets set up in each town along the route, despite being chilly at times. The lowest cost month to cruise the Rhine is November.

September is the ideal month to sail the Rhine, if we were to choose one. Why? With the remains of summer's warmth still in the air, fall foliage is transforming central Europe into a harvest wonderland. The season also has chilly autumn temperatures, making the attractions and locations much more enjoyable to explore due to the notably smaller number of travelers through Europe.

If you truly love the warm summertime weather or if you want to experience a particular event like the Rhine on Fire fireworks displays or the Christmas Markets all year long, then, of course, visiting in a different month can suit your tastes better.

Spring Rhine River Cruises

March, April, and May can be a terrific time to visit Europe to witness the landscape reviving in vivid colors, notably the tulip fields that characterize many sections of the Netherlands' countryside, even though water levels can be unpredictable during this time.

Summer Rhine River Cruises

The Rhine River region experiences its highest volume of tourism throughout the summer. You're in luck if you enjoy the heat because it can get above 100 degrees Fahrenheit. Peak season means that towns and tourist destinations are typically far more crowded. This isn't always a terrible thing, but for some it may be a hassle, especially in the summer when it's so hot outside. This is the ideal time to enjoy the sun on each riverboat's expansive deck.

Winter Market Cruises on the Rhine

These exclusive cruises in November and December showcase the Christmas Markets, a distinctive custom that has marked the holidays along the Rhine for generations. On your Rhine River cruise, every city and town you visit will have an Old Town decked out in exquisite traditional Christmas decorations. The markets are at the center of it all, offering visitors the chance to savor the tastes of heirloom holiday foods, locally made crafts as keepsakes, and festivities that highlight each town's unique cultural background. Remember that these are somewhat cooler months, so bring lots of warm clothing!

The cold, deep winter months of January and February are when Rhine River excursions aren't offered; river traveling in the spring returns in March.

Water Levels

Planning a river cruise in Europe? Be mindful of how the water levels could impact your itinerary. Riverboats may not be able to pass under bridges when water levels are too high, and they may not be able to navigate particular sections of the river for extended riverboats when water levels are too low. A lock along the river may not be operating properly, which could potentially result in a delay.

Regretfully, even for astute planners, it is impossible to forecast the water level when making a cruise reservation because it is primarily dependent on the weather for that year or even that month. Don't worry if high or low water levels cause problems for your voyage; cruise lines will either wait for the water to rise to a safe level before continuing with the itinerary or they will offer to use your riverboat as a hotel and transport you to the scheduled stops via luxury coach.

It is true that everyday showers and snowmelt during the spring increase the likelihood of flooding in March, April, and May. Lower water levels may result from drier summers beginning in August. These differ from year to year, and should there be any last-minute modifications to the river level schedule, your Adventure Life Rhine River consultant or cruise director will get in touch with you. In the rare event that a river becomes impassable because of high or low water, passengers are typically offered the option to take a bus to follow a similar itinerary and often connect with another river ship to continue their cruise on a portion of the river that is navigable.

Chapter 3: Preparing for the trip

Choosing The Right Accommodation

Choosing the appropriate accommodation for a Rhine River cruise is a crucial element in ensuring a memorable and enjoyable journey. Whether your preference leans towards a luxurious onboard experience or a comfortable base for exploring surrounding destinations, several factors merit consideration when determining the ideal accommodation for your Rhine River cruise.

1. Cruise Ship Amenities:

Diverse river cruise ships provide an array of amenities, encompassing onboard dining options, entertainment, wellness facilities, and excursion programs. Your accommodation choice should align with your preferences for onboard activities and services, such as spa treatments, fitness centers, or evening entertainment.

2. Cabin Types:

River cruise ships offer various cabin types, ranging from standard staterooms to luxurious suites. Selection criteria often include budget constraints, desired space, and preferred amenities. Suites often provide additional benefits, such as private balconies or butler service, enhancing comfort and luxury.

3. Location within the Ship:

The placement of your accommodation within the ship significantly influences your onboard experience. Considerations include views and tranquility levels, with cabins at the front or rear potentially offering different perspectives. Proximity to common areas, like dining rooms and lounges, and the potential for noise from engine or anchor operations are also factors.

4. Scenic Views:

For many travelers, panoramic views of the scenic Rhine River landscape are integral to the river cruise experience. Opt for cabins with balconies or large windows to maximize enjoyment of the passing scenery. Upper deck cabins often afford unparalleled views of the river and its picturesque surroundings.

5. Accessibility:

In case of mobility concerns, evaluate the accessibility of different cabin types and the ship's overall layout. Accessible cabins and the availability of elevators and other facilities are pivotal in ensuring a comfortable and convenient experience onboard.

6. Additional Inclusions:

Some accommodations offer extra perks, such as complimentary shore excursions, priority dining reservations, or dedicated concierge service. Consider these inclusions to enhance your overall cruise experience when comparing accommodation options.

7. Personal Preferences:

Ultimately, personal preferences play a significant role in choosing the right accommodation. Whether prioritizing spaciousness, private outdoor space, or exclusive amenities, align your choices with individual preferences and priorities.

In summary, when selecting the right accommodation for a Rhine River cruise, a thoughtful consideration of these factors will enable an informed decision aligned with your travel style, preferences, and budget. Careful evaluation of available options ensures the optimization of your Rhine River cruise experience, creating enduring memories along one of Europe's most iconic waterways.

Travel Insurance

Securing travel insurance stands as a crucial consideration for individuals embarking on a Rhine River cruise, particularly those with stops in Amsterdam. While river cruises are generally regarded as a secure and enjoyable mode of travel, the unforeseen can disrupt or necessitate the cancellation of a planned trip.

Typically encompassing a range of potential issues, travel insurance for a Rhine River cruise covers aspects such as trip cancellation or interruption, medical emergencies, lost or delayed luggage, and other unanticipated expenses. This insurance type offers passengers peace of mind, assuring them of financial protection in the event of travel-related challenges.

When procuring travel insurance for a Rhine River cruise, a meticulous consideration of the specific requirements and concerns of the journey is imperative. For instance, passengers may desire coverage for pre-existing medical conditions and any activities or excursions planned during stops in Amsterdam or other ports along the Rhine.

Beyond standard travel insurance coverage, passengers on a Rhine River cruise may find value in optional add-ons, such as "cancel for any reason" coverage, which provides heightened flexibility in responding to unexpected alterations in travel plans.

Equally important is a thorough review of the terms and conditions outlined in the travel insurance policy, including any exclusions or limitations. This scrutiny ensures a clear understanding of the extent of coverage, enabling passengers to make well-informed decisions regarding their insurance needs.

In essence, travel insurance extends invaluable protection to passengers on a Rhine River cruise, furnishing financial security and peace of mind as they navigate their journey through Amsterdam and beyond. By thoughtfully assessing their insurance requirements and selecting a policy that aligns with those needs, passengers can embark on their cruise with confidence, equipped to handle any challenges that may arise.

Money Saving Tips

Going on a Rhine river cruise sounds like a really fun idea! It means you get to travel through beautiful scenery and visit lovely places. To make your trip even better and not spend too much money, it's important to plan carefully and make smart financial choices. That's why we're sharing some simple tips to help you save money while still having an amazing time on your Rhine river cruise.

1. Advance Booking Strategies:

Securing your reservation well in advance stands as a prudent approach to optimizing cost-efficiency on a Rhine river cruise. Numerous cruise lines extend early booking incentives, thereby enabling travelers to capitalize on reduced cruise fares through meticulous planning and timely reservations.

2. Exploit Special Promotions:

Vigilance towards ongoing special promotions and offerings by cruise lines is paramount. These promotions may encompass discounted fares, onboard credits, or additional perks, presenting opportunities for financial savings on your Rhine river cruise.

3. Strategic Shoulder Season Travel:

Deliberating travel during the shoulder season, positioned between peak and off-peak periods, can yield substantial cost savings. Opting for a Rhine river cruise in the spring or fall, when weather conditions remain favorable and crowds are less dense, may translate to a more budget-friendly travel experience.

4. Thoroughly Compare Cruise Lines:

Exercise diligence in comparing different cruise lines rather than settling for the initial Rhine river cruise option. Variances in amenities, itineraries, and pricing among cruise lines necessitate a comprehensive research effort to identify the most favorable value proposition.

5. Consideration of Shorter Itineraries:

Contemplating a shorter Rhine river cruise itinerary can contribute to overall cost reduction. Reduced cruise duration may lead to lower expenses for onboard activities and excursions, potentially aligning with a more economical travel budget.

6. Embrace Package Deals:

Explore the availability of package deals offered by select travel agencies or cruise lines, integrating airfare, accommodations, and supplementary amenities with your Rhine river cruise. Opting for a comprehensive package can yield cost savings compared to individualized bookings for each travel component.

7. Mindful Management of Onboard Expenses:

Exercise caution and financial prudence with regard to onboard expenses during your Rhine river cruise. Mindfully budgeting for items such as drinks, specialty dining, and shore excursions is essential to avoid inadvertent overspending and maintain fiscal discipline throughout your journey.

Internet And Wifi Availability On Your River Cruise

The availability of internet services on Rhine river cruises can be variable, contingent upon the cruise line and the specific vessel in question. Numerous contemporary cruise ships are equipped with onboard Wi-Fi, affording passengers the opportunity to remain connected during their river voyage. However, it is imperative to recognize that the reliability and speed of internet access on a river cruise may not parallel the standards experienced on land.

Some cruise lines extend complimentary Wi-Fi access in designated public areas, such as lounges or restaurants, while others may impose charges for internet usage. Moreover, the speed and quality of the connection may fluctuate based on the ship's location along the river and the availability of satellite signals.

For individuals placing a premium on connectivity throughout their Rhine river cruise, prudent pre-booking inquiries with the cruise line are recommended. Potential topics of exploration include the cost associated with Wi-Fi access, the coverage areas within the ship, and any bundled offerings for multiple devices or extended usage.

It is important to acknowledge that, due to the remote nature of river cruising, there may be instances when the ship traverses through regions with limited or no internet coverage. Consequently, setting realistic expectations and planning ahead for essential online activities, such as checking emails or maintaining communication with acquaintances, is advisable.

While the internet availability on Rhine river cruises may not mirror the seamlessness of terrestrial experiences, numerous passengers appreciate the opportunity to disconnect from the digital realm. Engaging with the picturesque scenery and rich history of the Rhine valley becomes a pivotal aspect of the river cruising appeal, offering a distinctive and immersive travel experience.

Best Rhine Cruise Lines With Budgeting

For those considering Rhine River cruises, several esteemed options cater to diverse preferences and budget considerations. When selecting the most suitable Rhine River cruise company, factors such as cost, itinerary attractions, and the composition of your travel group should be carefully evaluated. Among the well-known cruise operators on the Rhine are Tauck Tours, Viking River Cruises, Avalon Waterways, Emerald Waterways, and Adventures by Disney.

Tauck Tours

Tauck Tours offers Rhine River cruises spanning 8 to 25 days, showcasing activities such as exclusive vineyard wine tastings, visits to medieval settlements, and entertainment in cities like Bucharest, Budapest, Prague, and Vienna. Pricing, ranging from $3,000 to $12,500 or more, is influenced by variables such as seasonality, itinerary length, included attractions, activities, and amenities. Notable highlights of Tauck's Rhine River offerings include Imperial Evening in a Vienna palace, private tours of historical sites, and interactive workshops by Tauck's "maestros."

Viking River Cruises

Viking River Cruises, known for its stylish Viking Longships, provides a range of Rhine River itineraries. With spacious accommodations, multiple dining options, and diverse onboard activities, Viking's cruises cover iconic cities along the Rhine. Prices typically range from $2,000 to $8,000, depending on included amenities and events. Highlights of Viking's Rhine River cruises include picturesque locations like Koblenz, Cologne, and the stunning Rhine Gorge.

Avalon Waterways

Avalon Waterways, recognized for its panoramic ships like the Avalon Envision, offers Rhine River trips featuring expansive views. The ships provide various dining options, onboard activities, and spacious suites with floor-to-ceiling windows. Avalon presents itineraries lasting from 4 to 24 days, with additional lodging and extension choices. Noteworthy highlights encompass guided tours of historical sites, hikes, and scenic routes through picturesque regions like the Rhine Gorge. Prices may vary, ranging from $2,000 to $8,000 or beyond.

Emerald Waterways

Emerald Waterways presents modern Rhine River cruises with options for active travelers, including bike and walking tours. The 8-day Rhine Explorer cruise, priced around $2,000 to $5,000 or more, offers diverse experiences. Highlights include visits to historical sites, hikes, and biking on the scenic Rhine River.

Adventures By Disney

Families seeking a uniquely tailored experience on the Rhine can opt for Disney's river cruises. The 8-day cruise includes excursions such as bike rides and visits to iconic locations. While Disney offers fewer options, their family-friendly packages start at approximately $4,000 to $6,000 or more. Highlights include visits to cities like Amsterdam, Strasbourg, and Basel, with family-oriented activities such as a Strudel-making session and castle tours.

Chapter 4: Food and Drink Options Offered Onboard

Embarking on a Rhine River cruise means you're in for some seriously good food! The dining experience is all about exploring different flavors from the regions along the Rhine. Every meal is carefully made to show off the unique tastes of each place you visit. So, whether you're into fancy wines or just want to try local dishes, this cruise has something for everyone.

But it's not just about the food, it's about the whole vibe. Imagine chowing down on delicious meals while looking out at the gorgeous riverside views. It's not just about the places you're visiting; it's about enjoying the Rhine River itself.

The menus on board are made with a lot of thought. Each dish tells a story and lets you connect with the traditions and flavors of the places you're exploring. Whether it's a classic German breakfast, a relaxed lunch with French influences, or a fancy dinner with a bit of everything, every time you eat is a chance to dive deeper into the culture and food of the Rhine region.

As you sail along the river, the food and drinks are a big part of the whole experience. There are great wines, local drinks, and a bit of everything to suit your taste. So, not only is the Rhine River cruise a journey, but it's also like a tasty adventure—full of flavors, cultures, and a chance to really get to know the food along the way.

Foods To Expect:

Breakfast:

- Freshly baked pastries and bread, including Croissants, pain au chocolat, Danish pastries, multigrain rolls, and whole wheat bread.
- Cheeses and cold cuts such as German varieties paired with prosciutto, salami, and smoked ham.
- Fresh fruits like juicy watermelon, pineapple, grapes, and mixed berries.

- Yogurt and granola featuring creamy Greek yogurt topped with honey and homemade granola.
- Cereals and muesli, encompassing cornflakes, bran flakes, chocolate cereal, and traditional Swiss muesli.
- Eggs, prepared as perfectly poached eggs Benedict, fluffy scrambled eggs with chives, or soft-boiled eggs with soldiers.
- Bacon and sausages, with crisp strips of applewood-smoked bacon and flavorful local sausages.
- Omelets made to order with fillings like sautéed mushrooms, diced bell peppers, Swiss cheese, and fresh herbs.
- Pancakes or Belgian waffles adorned with maple syrup, fresh berries, and whipped cream.
- Assortment of teas, freshly brewed coffee, and a selection of fruit juices.

Lunch:

- Soups such as hearty bowls of German potato soup or French onion soup.
- Salads like a classic Niçoise salad or a refreshing German cucumber salad.
- Sandwiches with fillings like smoked trout and horseradish cream, ham and Emmental cheese, or turkey and cranberry sauce.
- Pasta dishes like Alsatian spaetzle with a creamy mushroom sauce or classic Italian pasta with pesto.
- Seafood options such as grilled Rhine river fish or crispy fried shrimp with aioli.
- Meat dishes like sauerbraten with red cabbage, roasted pork with mustard sauce, or beef rouladen.
- Vegetarian and vegan choices like stuffed bell peppers, eggplant gratin, or vegetable curry.

- Desserts such as Black Forest cake, apple crumble with vanilla sauce, or a selection of fresh fruit.

Dinner:

- Multi-course gourmet meals featuring local and international cuisine.
- Regional specialties like Wiener schnitzel, Alsatian tarte flambée, Dutch herring, and Swiss cheese fondue.
- Fish and seafood options like grilled salmon from the Rhine, shrimp risotto, or Dutch mussels.
- Vegetarian and vegan entrees like stuffed vine leaves, vegetable lasagna, or Swiss potato rosti.
- Themed dinners such as Alsatian or Dutch nights featuring traditional dishes and live entertainment.

- Coffee and tea options post-dinner, including espresso, cappuccino, and herbal teas.

Drinks To Expect:

- Wine tastings showcasing local wines such as German Riesling, Alsatian Gewürztraminer, or Dutch white wines.
- Regional spirits like Dutch gin or German schnapps.

- Beer including German lagers, Dutch pilsners, and Alsatian bière de garde.
- Soft drinks such as cola, lemon-lime soda, and tonic water, along with non-alcoholic cocktails.
- Specialty coffee drinks like espresso and cappuccino.
- Bottled water.
- Fruit juices including apple, orange, and grape, typically available during meals.

Chapter 5: Sightseeing

Historic Sites Located Directly Along The Rhine River

In Basel, Switzerland

Basel is a lively city by the Rhine River, full of history and different cultures. It's in the middle of Switzerland, France, and Germany, so it has a mix of influences. Over the years, the city has changed a lot, and now it has many historic sites that share its story. When you walk through Basel's cozy streets and along the river, you'll find beautiful buildings and important cultural spots that highlight the city's long history. Here are some historic spots along the Rhine River in Basel:

1. Basel Minster (Basler Münster):

Dominating the city's skyline, the Basel Minster is a Gothic masterpiece and one of the most iconic landmarks in Basel. Construction of this cathedral began in the 12th century and continued for centuries. Visitors have the opportunity to ascend the towers, enjoying panoramic views of both the city and the Rhine. The Minster's intricate architecture and stunning stained glass windows make it a must-visit historic site.

2. Basel Rathaus (Town Hall):

The Basel Rathaus, or Town Hall, is a striking red sandstone building located on the banks of the Rhine. Built in the 16th century, it is a prime example of the Renaissance style. The exterior is adorned with colorful frescoes depicting historical events, and the interior features ornate rooms with intricate woodwork and period furnishings. Guided tours are available to explore the various chambers and halls.

3. Mittlere Brücke (Middle Bridge):

The Mittlere Brücke, or Middle Bridge, is one of Basel's oldest river crossings, spanning the Rhine. Although the current bridge is a reconstruction, it maintains its historic charm. The bridge provides a picturesque spot to enjoy views of the river and the surrounding cityscape.

In Strasbourg, France

Strasbourg, situated along the Rhine River in northeastern France, boasts a wealth of historic sites that contribute to its cultural and architectural appeal. Here are some notable historic sites in Strasbourg:

1. Strasbourg Cathedral (Cathédrale Notre-Dame de Strasbourg):

Strasbourg Cathedral, also known as Notre-Dame Cathedral, is a masterpiece of Gothic architecture. Its construction began in the 12th century, and the cathedral's intricate facade is adorned with sculptures and detailed carvings. The towering spire offers breathtaking views of the city and the Rhine Valley.

2. La Petite France:

La Petite France is a historic quarter in Strasbourg, characterized by charming half-timbered houses and narrow cobblestone streets. Dating back to the medieval and Renaissance periods, this area showcases the city's architectural heritage. The timber-framed houses, many of which have been preserved and restored, create a picturesque setting along the riverbanks.

3. Barrage Vauban (Vauban Dam):

The Barrage Vauban, a historic dam and bridge, was constructed in the 17th century by the military engineer Vauban. This strategic structure played a role in controlling water levels and defending the city. Today, it serves as both a functional bridge and an impressive architectural monument with panoramic views of Strasbourg and the surrounding waterways.

In Cologne and Düsseldorf - Germany

Cologne

Cologne is situated along the banks of the Rhine River, is home to several historic sites that contribute to the city's rich cultural and architectural heritage. Here are some notable historic sites in Cologne along the Rhine River:

1. Cologne Cathedral (Kölner Dom):

The Cologne Cathedral is one of Germany's most iconic landmarks and a UNESCO World Heritage

Site. Construction of this awe-inspiring Gothic masterpiece began in the 13th century, and it took centuries to complete. The cathedral's intricate facade, adorned with sculptures and gargoyles, dominates the city skyline. The panoramic views from the cathedral's towers provide a stunning perspective of the Rhine River and the surrounding city.

2. Hohenzollern Bridge (Hohenzollernbrücke):

Connecting the two banks of the Rhine, the Hohenzollern Bridge is a historic iron bridge with a distinctive appearance. Originally constructed in the early 20th century, the bridge was later rebuilt after World War II. What makes this bridge particularly famous is the thousands of love locks attached to its railings, symbolizing the enduring love of couples who visit Cologne.

3. Great St. Martin Church (Groß St. Martin):

Situated along the Rhine, the Great St. Martin Church is a Romanesque-style church with a history dating back to the 12th century. Despite being damaged during World War II, the church was meticulously restored, and its distinctive architecture, including four imposing towers, stands as a testament to Cologne's medieval past.

Düsseldorf

Düsseldorf is a city in Germany located on the beautiful Rhine River. It has a long history and several historic sites that show off the city's culture and past. Here are the some historic sites along the Rhine River in Düsseldorf you can find:

1. Schlossturm (Castle Tower):

The Schlossturm, also known as the Castle Tower, is a prominent medieval structure located on the banks of the Rhine. It is part of the Düsseldorf City Castle, which was built in the 13th century. The tower served various purposes throughout history, including as a watchtower, prison, and treasury. Today, the Schlossturm houses the Maritime Museum, offering visitors a glimpse into Düsseldorf's maritime history. The museum showcases a diverse collection of artifacts, ship models, and exhibits that narrate the city's connection to the Rhine River and its role in trade and navigation.

2. Rheinturm (Rhine Tower):

Although more modern than some other historic sites, the Rheinturm is a significant landmark along the Rhine River. Completed in 1982, this telecommunications tower stands at 240 meters and offers panoramic views of Düsseldorf and the surrounding areas. The tower's observation deck provides a unique perspective of the Rhine, the city's skyline, and even glimpses of the nearby historic landmarks. At night, the Rheinturm is illuminated, creating a stunning visual spectacle. The tower has become a symbol of Düsseldorf's modernity and a popular destination for both locals and tourists.

3. *Altstadt (Old Town):*

While not a single site, the Altstadt, or Old Town, along the Rhine River is a historic district that merits exploration. The area is characterized by narrow cobblestone streets, charming squares, and well-preserved medieval architecture. Key landmarks in the Altstadt include the Basilica St. Lambertus and the Schlossturm. The Old Town is not only a place to admire historical buildings but also a vibrant hub filled with lively pubs, restaurants, and shops. Locally known as the "longest bar in the world" due to its numerous pubs, the Altstadt is a perfect place to experience the city's lively atmosphere and taste traditional Altbier, the local beer.

Chapter 6: Languages Spoken in Some Neighboring Countries Along Rhine River

Languages Spoken in Switzerland With Some Phrases For Tourists

Switzerland is a country where people speak different languages. The country has four main languages: German, French, Italian, and Romansh. Most people in the central and eastern parts of the country speak German. They use a type of German called Swiss German, which is made up of different Alemannic dialects.

In the western part of Switzerland, in places like Geneva, Vaud, Neuchâtel, and Jura, people mostly speak French. Italian is spoken in the southern part of Switzerland, specifically in the canton of Ticino, which is close to Italy. Romansh, a Romance language, is spoken by a small number of people, mostly in the canton of Graubünden.

Having so many languages in Switzerland is a reflection of its rich cultural history and being close to many European countries. The mix of these languages has had a big impact on the traditions, customs, and how society works in Switzerland. It makes the country a special and diverse cultural mix in Europe. Here are some Romansh and Italian Phrases for tourists Switzerland:

Romansh Phrases

- Hello - Allegra (ah-LEH-grah)
- Good morning - Bun di (boon dee)
- Good evening - Buna saira (BOO-nah SAH-ee-rah)
- Good night - Buna notg (BOO-nah note)

- How are you? - Tge chaschien? (tgeh kah-SHEEN)
- I'm fine, thank you - Va bain, grischas (vah bine, GREE-shahs)
- What is your name? - Tge num sa chaschien? (tgeh noom sah kah-SHEEN)
- My name is... - Mia num ei... (mee-ah noom eye)
- Please - Per plaschair (pair PLAH-shai-er)
- Thank you - Grazia fitg (GRAH-tsee-ah feetg)
- You're welcome - Bitta, sgular (BEET-tah, SKOO-lahr)
- Yes - Gea (gheh-ah)
- No - Na (nah)
- Excuse me - Scusaziun (skoo-ZAH-tsee-oohn)
- I'm sorry - Excuses me (ex-KYOO-ses may)
- Goodbye - Buna notg (BOO-nah note) or See you later - A revair (ah reh-VEH-ar)

- I don't understand - Nagliu capir (NAH-lyoo kah-PEER)

- Can you help me? - Pumpastu m'agid? (POOM-pah-stoo mah-YEE)

- I need help - M'ajuda esser cumpartì (mah-YOO-dah ESS-ehr koom-par-TEE)

- How much does it cost? - Quant cascha? (kwahnt KAH-shah)

- Do you speak English? - Tgi era la englais? (gee eh-rah lah ayn-GLAYSS)

- I don't speak Romansh well - Nagliu parlar il rumantsch bain (NAH-lyoo pahr-LAHR eel roo-MAHNTSCH bine)

- What time is it? - Tge ura ei? (tgeh OO-rah eye)

- I am lost - Esser vi sin via (ESS-ehr vee seen VEE-ah)

- I need a taxi - M'alegra in taxi (mah-LEH-grah een TAHK-see)

Italian Phrases

- Hello - Ciao (chow)
- Good morning - Buongiorno (bwon-JOR-noh)
- Good evening - Buonasera (BWOH-nah-SEH-rah)
- Good night - Buona notte (BWOH-nah NOH-teh)
- How are you? - Come stai? (KOH-meh STAI?)
- I'm fine, thank you - Sto bene, grazie (STOH BEH-neh, GRAHTS-ee-eh)
- What is your name? - Come ti chiami? (KOH-meh tee KYAH-mee?)
- Please - Per favore (pehr fah-VOH-reh)
- Thank you - Grazie (GRAHTS-ee-eh)
- You're welcome - Prego (PREH-goh)
- Yes - Sì (see)
- No - No (noh)

- Excuse me - Mi scusi (mee SKOO-zee)

- I'm sorry - Mi dispiace (mee dees-pee-AH-cheh)

- Goodbye - Arrivederci (ah-ree-veh-DEHR-chee)

- Where is the bathroom? - Dov'è il bagno? (doh-VEH eel BAH-nyoh?)

- Can you help me? - Puoi aiutarmi? (pwah-ee ah-YOO-tar-mee?)

- I need help - Ho bisogno di aiuto (oh beezoh-NYOH dee ah-YOO-toh)

- How much does it cost? - Quanto costa? (KWAHN-toh KOH-stah?)

- Do you speak English? - Parli inglese? (PAHR-lee een-GLEH-zeh?)

- I don't speak Italian well - Non parlo bene l'italiano (non PAR-loh BEH-neh lee-tah-LYAH-noh)

- Do you have a menu in English? - Avete un menù in inglese? (ah-VEH-teh oon meh-NOO een een-GLEH-zeh?)
- What time is it? - Che ore sono? (keh OH-reh SOH-noh?)
- Where is the train station? - Dov'è la stazione ferroviaria? (doh-VEH lah stah-zee-OH-neh fehr-roh-VYAH-ryah?)
- I am lost - Mi sono perso/a (mee SOH-noh PEHR-soh/sah)
- I need a taxi - Ho bisogno di un taxi (oh bee-zoh-NYOH dee oon TAHK-see)
- It is beautiful here - È bellissimo qui (eh bel-LEE-see-moh kwee)
- I am from... - Sono di... (SOH-noh dee...)
- Have a nice day! - Buona giornata! (BWOH-nah JOR-nah-tah!)

Languages Spoken in Liechtenstein With Some Phrases For Tourists

In Liechtenstein, the official language is German, but it's a bit different from the standard High German. The German spoken there includes elements from Alemannic dialects, giving it a unique local flavor. This dialect is influenced by the cultural and historical context of Liechtenstein and shares similarities with the Swiss German spoken in nearby regions.

Even though German is the official language, many people in Liechtenstein also understand and speak English, especially in business and tourism. Additionally, because Liechtenstein is close to Austria and Switzerland, residents might also be familiar with and able to speak Austrian German and Swiss German dialects.

The language scene in Liechtenstein is mainly shaped by German, with its own local twist. However, there's also a practical use of English, and an awareness of regional dialects due to the country's geographical and historical connections with neighboring nations. Here are some German Phrases for tourists in Liechtenstein:

Liechtenstein German (Local Variations)

- Hello - Servus - (SER-voos)
- Goodbye - Auf Wiederschaun - (owf VEE-der-shawn)
- Please - Bitte - (BIH-te)
- Thank you - Danke - (DAHN-keh)
- How are you? - Wie geht's dir? - (vee gayt's deer)
- Good morning - Grias di - (gree-ahs dee)
- Good evening - Guata Obig - (GWAH-ta OH-big)

- What's your name? - Wie heißt du? - (vee hysst doo)

- I love you - I liab di - (ee leeb dee)

- Yes - Jo - (yoh)

- No - Nai - (nine)

- How much does it cost? - Wieviel koscht das? - (vee-feel kosht das)

- Where is the bathroom? - Wo isch's WC? - (vo ish's VAY-tsay)

- Where is the train station? - Wo isch dr Bahnhof? - (vo ish deer BAHN-hof)

- I don't understand - I verstoh nöd - (ee fer-shtoh nerd)

- I don't know - I weiss nöd - (ee vayss nerd)

- Can I help you? - Chan I dir hälfe? - (khan ee deer HEHL-fuh)

- That tastes good - Das schmöckt guet - (das shmuhkt GWAYT)

- Good night - Guata Nacht - (GWAH-ta NaKHt)

- What time is it? - Wie spät isch es? - (vee shpayt ish es)

- Where are you from? - Wo chunsch du här? - (vo khoonst doo hair)

- I am tired - I bin müed - (ee bin MYU-deh)

- Cheers! - Proscht! - (prohst)

- Good luck! - Viel Glück! - (feel glook)

- What are you doing? - Was machsch du? - (vahs MAKHSH doo)

- That is interesting - Das isch interessant - (das ish in-teh-res-sant)

- How is the weather? - Wie isch's Wetter? - (vee ish VET-ter)

- I'm happy - Ich freu mich - (ikh froy mish)

- Where is the supermarket? - Wo isch de Supermarkt? - (vo ish de soo-per-markt)

- What do you like to do? - Was machsch gärn? - (vahs MAKHSH gern)

Languages Spoken in Austria With Some Phrases For Tourists

The official language of Austria is German, but it's a bit different from the German spoken in Germany. The Austrian version, called Austrian German, includes various regional dialects and expressions influenced by history, culture, and geography, making it unique.

Apart from German, there are also other languages spoken in specific areas of Austria. These include Croatian, Hungarian, Slovenian, and Burgenland Croatian, which have historical ties and are spoken by minority groups.

Interestingly, many Austrians, especially in cities and among younger people, are good at English. English is commonly used in business, tourism, and talking with people from other countries. This mix of German, minority languages, and English shows Austria's diverse and open-minded culture, embracing different languages and global connections. Here are some Austrian German Phrases for tourists:

Austrian German Phrases

- Hello - Servus - (SER-voos)
- Goodbye - Auf Wiederschaun - (owf VEE-der-shawn)
- Please - Bitte - (BIH-te)
- Thank you - Danke - (DAHN-keh)
- You're welcome - Gern geschehen - (gern ge-SHAY-en)
- Excuse me/I'm sorry - Verzeihung - (fehr-TSAY-oong)
- How are you? - Wie geht's dir/Ihnen? - (vee gayt's deer/ihn-en)

- What's your name? - Wie heißt du/Sie? - (vee hysst doo/see)

- My name is... - I bin der/die... - (ee bin dare/dee...)

- Yes - Ja - (yah)

- No - Nein - (nine)

- I don't understand - I versteh das net - (ee fer-shtay das net)

- I don't know - I weiß nicht - (ee vays nikht)

- How much does it cost? - Wie viel kost't des? - (vee feel kostt des)

- Where is the bathroom? - Wo ist das WC? - (vo ist das VAY-tsay)

- I love you - I liab di - (ee leeb dee)

- Good morning - Grias di - (gree-ahs dee)

- Good afternoon - Guten Nachmittag - (GOO-ten NAHKH-mit-tahk)

- Cheers! - Prosit! - (proh-sit)

- Can I have the bill, please? - Die Rechnung, bitte. - (dee REKH-noong, BIH-te)

- Where is the train station? - Wo is da Bahnhof? - (vo is dah BAHN-hof)
- Do you speak English? - Reden Sie Englisch? - (RAY-den zee ENG-lish)
- I'm lost - I hob mi verirrt. - (ee hawb mee fehr-irt)
- I'm hungry - I bin hungerig. - (ee bin HOONG-rik)
- I'm thirsty - I bin durstig. - (ee bin DOOR-stig)

Languages Spoken in Germany With Some Phrases For Tourists

In Germany, the official language is German, and most people speak it. The standard form, called High German or Hochdeutsch, is used in writing and speaking officially. However, the language in Germany is not the same everywhere; there are many regional dialects and variations.

Different areas have their own dialects like Bavarian, Swabian, Saxon, and Low German (Plattdeutsch). These come with unique words, pronunciation, and grammar, showing the historical and cultural distinctions among German regions.

Besides the regional differences, Germany also has minority languages like Upper and Lower Sorbian, North Frisian, Saterland Frisian, and Low Rhenish. These languages are officially recognized and protected under European regulations supporting regional or minority languages.

Moreover, a lot of people in Germany, especially the younger generation and those in cities, are good at English. English is widely used in business, education, and tourism, adding to Germany's multilingual atmosphere.

The diverse linguistic landscape in Germany, with its regional dialects, minority languages, and proficiency in English, reflects the country's cultural and historical richness, as well as its active involvement in the globalized world. Here are some German Phrases for tourists in Germany:

Standard German Phrases

- Hello - Hallo - (HAH-lo)
- Goodbye - Auf Wiedersehen - (owf VEE-der-zay-en)
- Please - Bitte - (BIH-teh)
- Thank you - Danke - (DAHN-keh)
- How are you? - Wie geht es dir? - (vee geyt es deer)
- What's your name? - Wie ist dein Name? - (vee ist dine nah-meh)
- I love you - Ich liebe dich - (ikh lee-beh deekh)

- Yes - Ja - (yah)

- No - Nein - (nine)

- How much does it cost? - Wie viel kostet das? - (vee feel kos-tet das)

- Where is the bathroom? - Wo ist die Toilette? - (vo ist dee toy-LET-uh)

- Where is the train station? - Wo ist der Bahnhof? - (vo ist dare BAHN-hof)

- I don't know - Ich weiß nicht - (ikh vays nikht)

- Can I help you? - Kann ich Ihnen helfen? - (kahn ikh EEN-en hell-fen)

- That tastes good - Das schmeckt gut - (das shmekht goot)

- What time is it? - Wie spät ist es? - (vee shpet ist es)

- Where are you from? - Woher kommst du? - (VO-har kohmst doo)

- I am tired - Ich bin müde - (ikh bin MYU-deh)

- Cheers! - Prost! - (prohst)

- Good luck! - Viel Erfolg! - (feel er-folk)

- I look forward to it - Ich freue mich darauf - (ikh FROY-eh mikh dah-roof)

- That's fun - Das macht Spaß - (das makhed shpahss)

- I have a question - Ich habe eine Frage - (ikh HAH-beh I-ne frah-ge)

- Excuse me - Entschuldigung - (ent-SHOOL-di-gung)

- I am hungry - Ich bin hungrig - (ikh bin HOONG-rik)

- I am thirsty - Ich bin durstig - (ikh bin DOOR-stig)

- I am busy - Ich bin beschäftigt - (ikh bin be-shæf-tigt)

- The sun is shining - Die Sonne scheint - (dee ZOHN-neh shaynt)

- It's raining - Es regnet - (es RAYG-net)

- How is the weather? - Wie ist das Wetter? - (vee ist das VEHT-er)

- That is interesting - Das ist interessant - (das ist in-teh-res-sant)

- I am lost - Ich habe mich verirrt - (ikh HAH-beh mikh fehr-irt)

- That is easy - Das ist einfach - (das ist EEN-fakh)

- That is difficult - Das ist schwer - (das ist shvair)

- That is beautiful - Das ist wunderschön - (das ist VOON-der-shurn)

- I like that - Ich mag das - (ikh mahk das)

- I am happy - Ich bin glücklich - (ikh bin GLUKH-likh)

- I am sad - Ich bin traurig - (ikh bin TRAU-rikh)

- Good day - Guten Tag - (GOO-ten tahk)

Languages Spoken in France With Some Phrases For Tourists

The official language of France is French, which serves as the primary language of communication, administration, and education throughout the country. Standard French, also known as Metropolitan French, is based on the dialect of the Île-de-France region, particularly Paris, and is used as the norm for written and formal spoken communication.

However, France is also home to a rich array of regional languages and dialects, reflecting the country's diverse historical and cultural influences. These include languages such as Occitan, Breton, Alsatian, Basque, Corsican, and many others. While these languages do not have official status at a national level, they are recognized as part of

France's cultural heritage and are protected under regional language laws.

In addition to its regional diversity, France is also a country where English proficiency is increasingly prevalent, particularly among the younger population and those involved in international business, technology, and academia. English is commonly taught in schools and universities, and its usage as a second language has become more widespread in urban centers and tourist destinations. Here are some French Phrases for tourists:

French Phrases

- Hello - Bonjour (bohn-zhoor)
- Thank you - Merci (mehr-see)
- Goodbye - Au revoir (oh reh-vwahr)
- Yes - Oui (wee)

- No - Non (noh)

- Excuse me - Excusez-moi (ehk-skew-zay mwah)

- How are you? - Comment ça va? (koh-mah sah vah)

- Do you speak English? - Parlez-vous anglais? (par-leh voo ahn-gleh)

- How much does this cost? - Combien ça coûte? (kohm-byen sah koot)

- Cheers! - Santé! (sahn-tay)

- Have a good day - Bonne journée (bohn zhur-nay)

- Good night - Bonne nuit (bohn nwee)

- I'm sorry - Désolé(e) (day-zoh-lay)

- Where are you from? - D'où venez-vous? (doo vehn-ay voo)

- I am lost - Je suis perdu(e) (zhuh swee pair-doo)

- Help! - Aidez-moi! (eh-day mwah)
- Where is the train station? - Où est la gare? (oo eh lah gahr)
- I am hungry - J'ai faim (zhay fahng)
- I am tired - Je suis fatigué(e) (zhuh swee fah-tee-gay)
- What time is it? - Quelle heure est-il? (kell ur ay-teel)
- Can you help me? - Pouvez-vous m'aider? (poo-veh voo may-day)
- Nice to meet you - Enchanté(e) (ahn-shan-tay)
- I like that - J'aime ça (zhem sah)
- That's delicious! - C'est délicieux! (say day-lee-syuh)
- I need a taxi - J'ai besoin d'un taxi (zhay buh-zwahn duhn tahk-see)

- What is that? - Qu'est-ce que c'est? (kest kuh say)

Languages Spoken in Netherlands With Some Phrases For Tourists

The Netherlands officially speaks Dutch, with a formal version known as "Algemeen Beschaafd Nederlands" (General Civilized Dutch) used in education, media, and official communication. Despite this, the country boasts a varied linguistic scene rich in dialects and regional languages.

Alongside Standard Dutch, there are acknowledged regional languages and dialects found across the nation. Frisian, spoken in Friesland in the north, holds a unique status as both a recognized regional language and the second official language in the province. Its historical and linguistic roots make Frisian a vital part of the region's cultural identity.

Other regional languages and dialects, including Limburgish, Low Saxon, and various local dialects, reflect historical and cultural distinctions between provinces and regions. While these languages lack national official status, they are treasured as crucial elements of the country's linguistic heritage.

In addition to native languages, English proficiency is widespread in the Netherlands, particularly among the younger population and in urban areas. English finds common usage in business, education, and tourism, reflecting the country's international outlook and engagement.

The Netherlands' linguistic diversity, comprising Standard Dutch, regional languages, and English proficiency, mirrors the nation's rich heritage, regional identities, and global connections. The coexistence of these languages and dialects underscores the Netherlands' cultural complexity and its openness to linguistic diversity. Here are some Dutch Phrases for tourists:

Dutch Phrases

- Hello - Hallo (hah-loh)
- Good morning - Goedemorgen (hu-dah-mor-hen)
- Good afternoon - Goedemiddag (hu-dah-mi-dahk)
- Good evening - Goedenavond (hu-dah-nah-vont)
- Goodbye - Tot ziens (tot zeens)
- Please - Alsjeblieft (als-ye-bleeft)
- You're welcome - Graag gedaan (hrahkh huh-dahn)
- Yes - Ja (yah)
- No - Nee (nay)
- Maybe - Misschien (miss-kheen)
- Sorry - Sorry (sor-ree)

- How are you? - Hoe gaat het? (hoo gaat het?)
- Please - Alstublieft (ahl-stoo-bleeft)
- I don't understand - Ik begrijp het niet (ik buh-greip het neet)
- Do you speak English? - Spreekt u Engels? (spraykt uu en-khels?)
- How much does this cost? - Hoeveel kost dit? (hoo-vehl kost dit?)
- What is your name? - Wat is uw naam? (vat is uu naam?)
- What time is it? - Hoe laat is het? (hoo laht is het?)
- I am lost - Ik ben verdwaald (ik ben vur-dwahld)
- I need help - Ik heb hulp nodig (ik heb hulp no-dikh)
- What is the weather today? - Wat is het weer vandaag? (vat is het vayr van-dahkh?)

Chapter 7: Activities

Recommended itinerary for first time Tourists

Embarking on a Rhine River cruise is a delightful way to explore the heart of Europe, as it winds through picturesque landscapes, charming villages, and historic cities. Below is a recommended 8-day itinerary for first-timers on a Rhine River cruise, covering some of the most iconic and enchanting destinations along the way:

Day 1: Amsterdam, Netherlands

- Start your journey in the vibrant city of Amsterdam. Explore its iconic canals, visit the Anne Frank House, and wander through the historic Jordaan district.

- Board your cruise ship in the afternoon and settle into your cabin.
- Attend a welcome dinner on board as you set sail.

Day 2: Cologne, Germany

- Arrive in Cologne and visit the famous Cologne Cathedral (Kölner Dom), a UNESCO World Heritage Site.
- Explore the city's Old Town, with its charming shops, cafes, and the historic Rathaus (City Hall).

Day 3: Koblenz and the Middle Rhine

- Cruise to Koblenz, where the Rhine meets the Moselle River. Visit the Deutsches Eck (German Corner) and take a cable car to the Ehrenbreitstein Fortress for panoramic views.

- Cruise through the scenic Middle Rhine, known for its picturesque castles and vineyards.

Day 4: Rüdesheim and Rhine Gorge

- Explore Rüdesheim, a charming wine town. Visit the Siegfried's Mechanisches Musikkabinett, a museum of automated musical instruments.
- Cruise through the stunning Rhine Gorge, passing Lorelei Rock and numerous castles.

Day 5: Heidelberg

- Disembark in Heidelberg and visit the famous Heidelberg Castle, perched above the Neckar River.
- Stroll through the historic Old Town and visit the University of Heidelberg, one of the oldest universities in Europe.

Day 6: Strasbourg, France

- Cruise to Strasbourg, a picturesque city with a blend of French and German influences.
- Explore the UNESCO-listed Old Town, visit Strasbourg Cathedral, and take a boat tour along the canals.

Day 7: Breisach and Black Forest

- Dock in Breisach and choose between a visit to the Black Forest or a wine tasting excursion in the Alsace region.
- Explore the charming Black Forest villages or visit the cuckoo clock shops.

Day 8: Basel, Switzerland

- Conclude your cruise in Basel, Switzerland.
- Explore the city's Old Town, visit the Basel Minster, and stroll along the Rhine River promenade.

- Optional extension: Spend additional time in Switzerland or explore nearby cities like Zurich or Lucerne.

This itinerary provides a balance of cultural exploration, scenic cruising, and historical sightseeing, offering first-time visitors a rich and diverse experience along the Rhine River. Keep in mind that cruise itineraries may vary, so always check with your cruise provider for the most up-to-date information.

Shopping and Souvenirs with Insider's Tips

Going on a Rhine River cruise is a thrilling adventure, and buying souvenirs can be a really enjoyable part of your trip. The Rhine River runs through beautiful scenery and historic towns, providing a special shopping experience for those doing it for the first time. Below is a detailed guide on what you can anticipate and what kinds of souvenirs you might want to get.

General Shopping Tips:

1. Currency and Payment:

Before you start shopping, familiarize yourself with the local currency. In the Rhine River region, you might encounter different currencies depending on the countries you visit, such as the Euro in Germany and France.

2. Local Customs and Etiquette:

Be aware of local customs and etiquettes while shopping. Politeness and a few basic phrases in the local language can go a long way.

3. Best Time to Shop:

Explore local markets during your shore excursions. These are often held in the mornings, offering fresh produce, crafts, and unique items.

4. Bargaining:

Bargaining is not common in most European countries, including those along the Rhine. However, it's acceptable in some markets, especially if you're purchasing from smaller, independent vendors.

Souvenir Ideas:

1. Wine and Spirits:

The Rhine is renowned for its vineyards and wineries. Consider purchasing local wines, such as Riesling from the German regions. Look for specialty spirits like schnapps or local liqueurs.

2. Cuckoo Clocks and Wooden Crafts:

In the Black Forest region, which the Rhine passes through, you can find traditional cuckoo clocks and beautifully crafted wooden items.

3. Chocolate and Confectionery:

Switzerland, often part of Rhine River itineraries, is famous for its chocolate. Indulge in high-quality Swiss chocolates or look for local confectioneries in other stops along the way.

4. Ceramics and Pottery:

Rhineland is known for its pottery and ceramics. Look for hand-painted plates, cups, and other decorative items that showcase the craftsmanship of the region.

5. Local Art and Crafts:

Visit art galleries or craft shops in towns along the Rhine. You might find paintings, sculptures, or handmade crafts that reflect the local culture.

6. Cologne Fragrance:

If your cruise takes you to Cologne in Germany, consider purchasing the famous "Eau de Cologne." This fragrance originated here, and you can find a variety of scented products.

7. Antiques and Vintage Finds:

Explore antique shops in quaint towns along the river. You might discover unique vintage items that carry a piece of local history.

8. Local Apparel and Textiles:

Invest in traditional clothing or textiles unique to the region. This could include scarves, shawls, or garments made from local fabrics.

Where to Shop:

1. Markets:

Visit local markets in towns like Strasbourg, Cologne, or Basel. These markets offer a vibrant atmosphere with a variety of products, from fresh produce to handmade crafts.

2. Boutiques and Specialty Stores:

Explore boutique shops in historic town centers. These stores often carry curated selections of high-quality, locally made goods.

3. Artisan Workshops:

Seek out artisan workshops where craftsmen create and sell their products. This provides an opportunity to see the crafting process and purchase one-of-a-kind items.

4. Duty-Free Shops:

Check the duty-free shops onboard your cruise ship for a selection of souvenirs and gifts.

Chapter 8: Exploring Some Neighboring Rivers Along Rhine River

Overview Of Meuse River

The Meuse River, known as Maas in Dutch, meanders through Western Europe, covering about 575 miles (925 kilometers) across France, Belgium, and the Netherlands. Originating in Pouilly-en-Bassigny, France, it takes a northward course, ultimately emptying into the North Sea near Rotterdam. Beyond its extensive length, the Meuse plays a pivotal role in the history, culture, and economic vitality of the regions it traverses.

The river's journey unfolds a diverse tapestry of landscapes. In France, it winds through the picturesque Ardennes region, characterized by hilly terrains and dense forests. As it flows into Belgium, the Meuse graces cities like Dinant and Namur, carving through steep cliffs and fertile valleys. Upon entering the Netherlands, the river reveals extensive floodplains and fertile agricultural land, showcasing a mosaic of environments along its course.

However, the Meuse is not just a geographic feature. Its banks bear witness to centuries of history, adorned with castles, forts, and ancient towns. The echoes of past battles, particularly from World War I and II, resonate in the historical narratives woven into the Meuse's waters and its surroundings.

Nature finds refuge along the Meuse, where diverse flora and fauna thrive in wetlands and floodplain forests. The conservation of these habitats is crucial to maintaining the river's ecological richness. The Meuse River is more than a waterway; it is a living testimony to the interconnectedness of geography, history, and ecology.

Notably, the Meuse shares a connection with the Rhine River. In the Netherlands, near Rotterdam, these two rivers converge in a delta, forming a complex water system. This confluence holds historical and economic significance, influencing trade, transportation, and water resource utilization in the region.

This River weaves together the landscapes, history, and ecosystems of Western Europe. Its journey, marked by diverse terrains and historical landmarks, is a testament to the intricate interplay of geography and human influence. Additionally, its connection with the Rhine River adds another layer to the complexity and importance of this watercourse in the region.

Overview Of Moselle River

The Moselle River, known as Mosel in German, gracefully winds its way through the picturesque landscapes of France, Luxembourg, and Germany, spanning approximately 545 kilometers (339 miles). As a tributary of the Rhine, this river is celebrated for its breathtaking scenery, historic towns, and flourishing wine industry.

Originating in the Vosges mountains of northeastern France near the village of Bussang, the Moselle embarks on a northeast journey, passing through the French Lorraine region and being joined by tributaries like the Meurthe and the Madon. It serves as a natural border between Luxembourg and Germany before entirely flowing within Germany and meeting the Rhine at Koblenz.

One of the Moselle's most enchanting features is its stunning landscape. The river traverses a valley bordered by steep slopes adorned with vineyards, creating a spectacular and romantic vista. Renowned for its wine production, especially white wines, the Moselle's vineyards attract wine enthusiasts and tourists alike.

The towns and cities along the Moselle River are steeped in history and charm. Trier, Germany's oldest city, sits on the riverbanks, showcasing well-preserved Roman ruins, including the UNESCO World Heritage Site Porta Nigra. Other notable towns like Bernkastel-Kues and Cochem exude medieval architecture, half-timbered houses, and a distinctly romantic ambiance.

As a significant transportation route, the Moselle has played a vital role in facilitating trade and commerce throughout history. Beyond its economic impact, the river has inspired artists and writers drawn to its idyllic setting and cultural richness.

From an ecological standpoint, the Moselle and its surrounding region harbor diverse flora and fauna. The river and its floodplains provide habitats for various plant species, birds, and aquatic life. Ongoing efforts to conserve and protect the natural environment of the Moselle recognize the importance of preserving the ecological balance of the river and its surroundings.

The Moselle River's connection to the Rhine adds to the overall significance of the region's waterways. In Koblenz, where the Moselle meets the Rhine, a notable confluence occurs, influencing the surrounding landscapes, history, and economic activities. This interconnectedness of rivers contributes to the rich tapestry of Western Europe, highlighting the integral role watercourses play in shaping the character and heritage of the region.

Overview Of Main River

The Main River, pronounced "mine" in English, stands as a significant waterway in Germany, weaving through vital cities and landscapes with a length of approximately 525 kilometers (326 miles). As a tributary of the Rhine, the Main River plays a pivotal role in the economic, cultural, and historical development of the region.

Originating in the Franconian Rhon mountains in Bavaria, Germany, the Main River flows northward, gracing cities like Bamberg, Wurzburg, Aschaffenburg, and Frankfurt before merging with the Rhine at Mainz. Its diverse landscapes, featuring vineyard-covered hills, historic towns, and bustling urban centers, contribute to the Main River's distinctive character.

A defining attribute of the Main River is its historical importance in trade and transportation. Throughout the ages, it has served as a vital waterway, fostering the movement of goods, people, and ideas. The cities along its course have thrived as hubs of commerce and culture, owing much of their prosperity to the navigable waters of the Main River.

The Main River valley, particularly around Wurzburg, is celebrated for its wine production. The region's vineyards, clinging to the slopes along the river, produce high-quality white wines, attracting wine enthusiasts and tourists. The combination of rolling vineyards, historic towns, and the meandering river crafts a captivating and picturesque landscape.

Beyond its economic significance, the Main River has played a central role in shaping the history and cultural heritage of the region. Along its banks, visitors encounter architectural and historical landmarks, including medieval castles, baroque palaces, and well-preserved old towns. Cities like Wurzburg and Frankfurt showcase a rich cultural tapestry, blending historic charm with modern vibrancy.

From an environmental standpoint, the Main River and its surroundings host diverse ecosystems and wildlife. Conservation efforts have been implemented to preserve the natural habitats along the river, emphasizing sustainable development and the protection of the diverse flora and fauna that call the Main River home.

In considering the interconnected waterways of the region, the Main River, as a tributary of the Rhine, contributes to the broader narrative of Western Europe's rivers playing integral roles in shaping landscapes, fostering commerce, and preserving cultural heritage.

Overview Of Neckar River

The Neckar River is a really important river in southwest Germany. It's like a lifeline for the towns and cities along its 367-kilometer journey. It starts in the Black Forest and goes through places like Tübingen, Stuttgart, Heilbronn, and Mannheim, where it meets the Rhine River. The Neckar River has been crucial for the history, culture, and economy of the area.

This river is special because it has a long history. The towns and cities along it have old buildings, castles, and forts that show how important the river was for trade and mixing cultures. The Neckar River has been helpful for moving things around, which helped the towns and cities grow.

The area around the Neckar River is really beautiful. There are hills covered in vineyards, green forests, and cute towns. People here have been making wine for a really long time, and the vineyards along the river make great-quality wines.

The Neckar River also helps with industries. It used to help move goods through cities like Stuttgart and Heilbronn, helping the region grow. Even now, the Neckar River is still used to transport things, both for businesses and for fun activities.

A cool thing about the Neckar River is that it connects with the Rhine River. In Mannheim, they come together, and this connection is important for the region. It affects the landscapes and how people trade and travel in the area. Both rivers work together to make southwest Germany a special place.

Overview Of Ruhr River

The Ruhr River, also called Ruhr in German, is not like a usual river. Instead, it's a significant part of the

Rhine River system flowing through the Ruhr district in western Germany. The Ruhr region, especially the Ruhr Valley, has been crucial in Germany's history and economy, especially during the time when industries were growing.

The "Ruhr" comes together when several rivers, like the Ruhr, Lenne, Volme, and Möhne, join. This mix of rivers played a big role in building cities and industries in the area, especially during the industrial revolution.

From an industry point of view, the Ruhr Valley became a major place for making coal and steel in Europe during the 1800s and 1900s. The river and its smaller rivers helped move materials and finished products, making the region's industries grow. Cities like Dortmund, Essen, Duisburg, and Bochum became well-known for their industries, thanks to the resources and structures provided by the Ruhr River system.

The culture and history of the Ruhr River and its surroundings are closely linked to its industrial past. The big factories, steelworks, and mines not only changed the way the place looked but also influenced how people lived and thought. Even though industries have changed in recent years, there are efforts to keep and reuse old industrial places as cultural sites and places for new ideas.

Apart from its industrial role, the Ruhr River and the nearby areas have places with natural beauty in the middle of all the buildings. Green areas, parks, and turning old industrial places into fun spots provide a balance to the region, offering chances for people to relax and enjoy cultural things.

The Ruhr River is important not just for industry and history but also as a symbol for the people and communities there. The way locals have faced changes in industry, showing resilience and creativity, has become a big part of the area's pride and identity.

Chapter 9: Exploring the top Neighboring Cities Along Rhine River With Maps

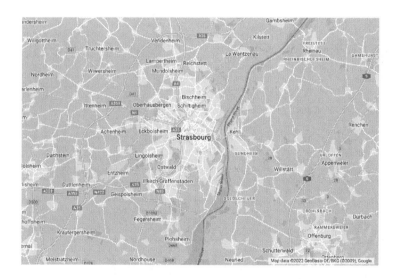

Overview Of Strasbourg with Tourist Map

Strasbourg is a city in northeastern France near Germany. It's the main city in the Grand Est region.

Strasbourg is important for its mix of French and German history, its old buildings, and its European identity. The city has a lot of history, and it's known for its unique character. Strasbourg is often talked about in European politics and culture.

The old part of the city is called "Grande Ile" (Grand Island) and is a UNESCO World Heritage site. It has old buildings, narrow streets, and wooden houses. The big Cathedral of Our Lady of Strasbourg is a symbol of the city. It has a tall, pointy roof and offers great views from the top.

Strasbourg is in a good spot, between the Rhine River, which is a big river in Europe, and it's a place where France and Germany connect. This has made Strasbourg important for business, talking between countries, and sharing cultures. The city has a mix of French and German ways, making a unique identity called Alsatian.

In the European Union, Strasbourg is like a headquarters. Important EU groups, like the European Parliament and the European Court of Human Rights, have their offices there. This makes Strasbourg a symbol of countries in Europe working together.

Strasbourg is not just about politics; it's also a lively place for art. There are many museums, theaters, and galleries showing different types of art. The food in Strasbourg is a mix of French and German too, with dishes like sauerkraut with sausages and a kind of thin-crust pizza.

The Christmas market in Strasbourg is very famous and old, attracting people from everywhere. It has a happy feel with traditional crafts and tasty seasonal treats. Strasbourg tries hard to keep its traditions alive, especially during Christmas, making it a special place to visit during the holiday season.

Strasbourg is a city with a mix of history, culture, and importance today. It shows how France and Germany have influenced each other and how Europe can work together. The beautiful buildings, lively culture, and political importance make Strasbourg a fascinating place that represents the heart of Europe.

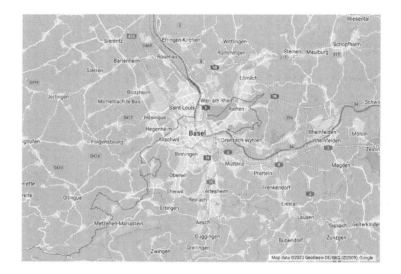

Overview Of Basel with Tourist Map

Basel, a city in Switzerland near the borders of Germany and France, is a significant cultural and economic center. It's known for its rich history, diverse culture, and strategic location at the meeting point of three countries.

The city boasts a mix of influences from Switzerland, Germany, and France, creating a unique identity. Basel has a long history, with well-preserved old buildings and a charming old town that reflects its medieval roots.

Culturally, Basel is a vibrant hub with numerous museums, art galleries, and theaters. The city is home to the renowned Art Basel fair, one of the leading international art fairs. This event attracts artists, collectors, and art enthusiasts from around the world.

Basel's location on the Rhine River has historically made it a crucial center for trade and commerce. The city has a strong economy and is a hub for the pharmaceutical and chemical industries. The presence of international organizations and financial institutions further contributes to Basel's economic significance.

In addition to its economic and cultural aspects, Basel is known for its commitment to sustainability and environmental consciousness. The city places a strong emphasis on green initiatives and has earned a reputation as an environmentally friendly destination.

With its blend of history, culture, economic strength, and environmental consciousness, Basel stands as a dynamic city that bridges the gap between different cultures and nations, making it a compelling destination in the heart of Europe.

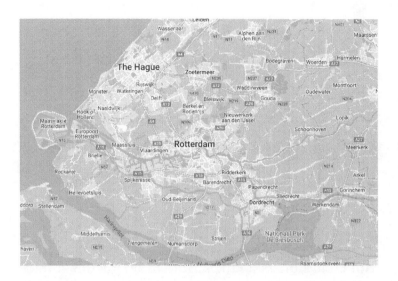

Overview Of Rotterdam with Tourist Map

Rotterdam, a major port city in the Netherlands, is a bustling and modern metropolis with a unique character. Located in the southwestern part of the country, Rotterdam stands out for its contemporary architecture, vibrant cultural scene, and maritime importance.

The city has a distinctive skyline featuring innovative and modern buildings, a result of extensive reconstruction after World War II. Rotterdam is known for its architectural diversity and has become a showcase for cutting-edge design and urban planning.

As one of the largest and busiest ports in Europe, Rotterdam plays a crucial role in international trade and commerce. The port is a hub for goods coming in and out of Europe and contributes significantly to the city's economic strength.

Culturally, Rotterdam offers a diverse range of attractions, including museums, galleries, and theaters. The city is home to the Boijmans Van Beuningen Museum, showcasing an extensive art collection, and the iconic Cube Houses, a unique residential complex designed in a distinctive cube shape.

Rotterdam's commitment to sustainability is evident in its efforts to create a greener and more environmentally friendly urban environment. The city has implemented various initiatives to enhance sustainability, such as green spaces, eco-friendly architecture, and sustainable transportation options.

The multicultural atmosphere in Rotterdam adds to its appeal, with a diverse population and a thriving international community. The city hosts various events and festivals that celebrate its cultural diversity and creative energy.

In summary, Rotterdam is a dynamic city that blends modernity with maritime heritage. Its striking architecture, economic significance, cultural vibrancy, and commitment to sustainability make it a compelling destination in the Netherlands and a key player on the European stage.

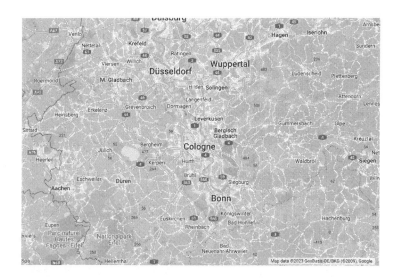

Overview Of Cologne with Tourist Map

Cologne, a city in western Germany along the Rhine River, is a vibrant and historic metropolis known for its rich cultural heritage and iconic landmarks. This bustling city seamlessly combines its ancient roots with a lively contemporary atmosphere.

Cologne is famous for its stunning cathedral, the Cologne Cathedral, or Kölner Dom, a masterpiece of Gothic architecture. This UNESCO World Heritage site is not only a symbol of the city but also one of the most visited landmarks in Germany. Its towering spires dominate the skyline and showcase the city's historical significance.

With a history dating back over 2,000 years, Cologne has preserved its medieval charm in the Altstadt (Old Town). Narrow cobblestone streets, colorful houses, and lively squares create a picturesque setting for locals and visitors alike. The city's historic roots are also reflected in Romanesque churches and ancient city gates.

As a major cultural hub, Cologne offers a diverse array of museums, galleries, and theaters. The city hosts various cultural events and festivals throughout the year, drawing artists and enthusiasts from around the world. The Museum Ludwig, for instance, features an impressive collection of modern art, including works by Picasso and Warhol.

Cologne's position as a transportation hub, particularly as a key location along the Rhine River, has contributed to its economic significance. The city is a major center for trade and industry and is known for its welcoming atmosphere for businesses and innovation.

Cologne's cultural diversity is evident in its lively neighborhoods, each with its unique character. The city's open-minded and friendly atmosphere is celebrated in events such as the Cologne Carnival, one of the largest street festivals in Europe, where locals and visitors come together to enjoy parades and festivities.

Chapter 10 : Health and Safety Precautions

Safety Precautions

Making sure everyone stays safe is super important on a Rhine river cruise. The folks in charge of the cruise, like the crew and staff, do a bunch of things to keep everyone safe, both on the boat and when folks go on trips during the cruise.

First off, when the cruise starts, they make sure everyone knows what to do in case something unexpected happens. This means having mandatory drills to practice using life jackets, knowing where to go in case of an emergency, and where to meet up with others. The crew members are there to help and make sure everyone understands what to do if something comes up.

The boat itself is decked out with fancy navigation tools and safety gadgets to make sure it sails smoothly along the Rhine river. The crew members get serious training to handle any tricky situations that might pop up while cruising.

And hey, the people running the cruise have to follow strict rules from the folks who make sure everything at sea stays safe. They regularly check out the boats, make sure they follow all the international safety rules, and do what they're supposed to according to the local laws in the countries the cruise goes through.

When folks go on trips during the cruise, they get the lowdown on staying safe too. This means tips on sticking together, being aware of what's going on around them, and following any safety rules from the cruise or local authorities.

If something goes wrong, the boat has top-notch communication systems to quickly get help, and the crew members are trained to give first aid and medical help if needed.

Security On Excursion

When you're off the boat exploring during a Rhine river cruise, making sure everyone stays safe is really important. The people in charge of the cruise take a bunch of steps to make sure passengers can enjoy their time on land without any worries.

Initially, they make sure there are knowledgeable guides who know the area well. These guides work for the cruise line or are carefully chosen to make sure they're experts and act professionally.

Before passengers head off on land, they get important info about staying safe. This might include sticking together, being aware of what's happening around them, and following any safety tips from the cruise or local authorities. They also learn where and when to meet back up with the ship to make sure no one gets left behind.

The cruise line works closely with local authorities to keep things secure during these trips. This could mean talking to the police, security folks, or other important groups to make sure everything is safe and sound while passengers check out the different spots along the Rhine river.

Sometimes, the cruise line adds extra safety measures, like having security people around, especially in places where there might be some safety concerns, like busy tourist areas or cities with a history of small crimes.

If there's ever a safety worry or an emergency during a trip, passengers are told to let their guide or a crew member know right away. The cruise ship has fancy communication systems to quickly get help and coordinate any necessary actions.

Emergency services

On a Rhine river cruise, keeping passengers safe in case of unexpected situations is a top priority. The cruise companies take careful steps to make sure that passengers not only have access to emergency services but also get quick and helpful assistance when needed.

One crucial emergency service on these cruises is medical help. The cruise ships have medical facilities and skilled medical staff ready to provide immediate care if someone gets sick or injured. These facilities are set up to handle minor health issues and can stabilize patients until they can be transferred to a local hospital.

If there's a medical emergency, passengers can quickly contact the ship's reception or crew members for immediate help. The crew is well-trained to respond to medical emergencies, swiftly getting the right medical personnel and resources to assist passengers in need.

Beyond medical assistance, the cruise companies work closely with local authorities and emergency services to make sure passengers have access to a full range of emergency support. This involves coordination with local hospitals, ambulances, and other emergency response agencies to ensure passengers can get the necessary care during emergencies.

Passengers are usually given important contact information for emergency services at each stop along the Rhine river. This includes details for local hospitals, emergency hotlines, and other necessary services. If there's a need for immediate medical help on board, passengers can contact the ship's reception.

In case of an emergency, passengers are told to quickly inform the ship's crew, who can rapidly organize the needed resources and work with local authorities to provide assistance. River cruise ships have advanced communication systems, making it easy to alert emergency services and coordinate response efforts efficiently.

Conclusion

Let the "Rhine River Cruise Travel Guide" be your compass through the timeless beauty of the Rhine. As you turn the final pages, envision not just a collection of destinations but a tapestry of moments etched into your soul. This guide is more than a travel companion; it's the key to unlocking a river odyssey where history, culture, and natural wonders converge. So, embrace the magic, savor the journey, and let the Rhine weave its indelible charm into the very fabric of your memories. Your adventure awaits – may it be as boundless as the river itself.